Talking About Writing

Part Two

**A sequential programme of
sentence structure, grammar,
usage and punctuation
for grade 9**

with accompanying *Answer Key*

"A little learning is a dangerous thing;"
(Alexander Pope, *Essay on Criticism*)

Let's drink more deeply of the Pierian spring.

Shirley Campbell, B.A., M.A.

Acknowledgements

Special thanks to Karl Bensmiller, *Computer Solutions Specialists*
Armstrong, British Columbia

and to Ernie Sollid, Computer Coordinator
School District 83, British Columbia

Order this book online at www.trafford.com
or email orders@trafford.com

Most Trafford titles are also available at major online book retailers.

Print information available on the last page.

ISBN: 978-1-5521-2246-4 (sc)

Trafford rev. 01/20/2023

North America & international
toll-free: 844-688-6899 (USA & Canada)
fax: 812 355 4082

Introduction

Talking about Writing is for high school teachers and students who

      l. need a common vocabulary with which to discuss written language;

      2. desire a working knowledge of the chief elements of sentence structure, grammar, usage and punctuation as they apply to the writing process;

      3. demand an integrated approach, and a sequenced format adaptable to individual lessons; and

      4. appreciate the help of an *Answer Key.*

A mechanic immersed in the intricacies of engine repair does not ask for a "thingummy" or a "whatsit." He or she names the tool and holds out a hand to receive it.

In the same way, teachers and students poring over the products of the writing process need **a basic common vocabulary** with which to discuss the work. They need to make mutually understandable statements which will clarify and improve the material under review. For example, "This sentence contains a misplaced modifier" is more helpful and precise than "Don't you think putting this bit in a different place will make the sentence sound better?" *Talking about Writing* supplies this basic vocabulary.

The text has a simple format. It teaches the recognition of the **nine sentence errors** which writers commonly make. **It integrates the grammar** necessary to understand each sentence error. **Sentence combining, usage, and punctuation exercises** strengthen writing technique.

Talking about Writing fills a need for both a concrete objective in English language study and **a teaching plan**. It provides a method of entry - the nine sentence errors - which is useful to many: beginning teachers, for example; teachers of other subjects who have been asked to pick up one or two blocks of English in the timetable; teachers who wish a clear explanation of the language in the writing process; or parents who run **home school**.

A further advantage is to **make a connection between the teaching of English language and other languages**; such as, French or Spanish. Students studying a second language are expected to recognize, for example, a direct object or a past participle in order to make the necessary agreement. The grammar component accompanying each sentence error encourages the transfer of this knowledge from one language to another.

Introduction, continued

Talking about Writing **is sequenced and self-explanatory**. In each chapter the material progresses in simple and logical increments to the desired end; namely, to recognize a sentence error in order to discuss written work, practise effective writing techniques, and empower communication. The sentence errors progress in difficulty from grades 8 to 12. **The format is adapted for individual lessons**.

Curriculum guides tend to be written in generalities. *Talking about Writing* **provides the teacher with a pattern**. Having experienced the focus of this programme and the integration of the topics, he or she then knows how to access additional material to suit a student's individual needs.

How *Talking about Writing* is Organized

Students are taught to recognize the nine major sentence errors: two in each of grades 8 to 11, and one in grade 12, as follows:

Grade 8 -   Run-on Sentence
            Sentence Fragment

Grade 9 -   Lack of Parallel Structure
            Misplaced Modifier

Grade 10 - Dangling Participle
            Lack of Agreement

Grade 11 - Indefinite Antecedent
            Incorrect Tense

Grade 12 - Wordiness

The grammar necessary to understand the sentence error is integrated with appropriate punctuation and sentence combining techniques.

A pre-test and a post-test accompany each sentence error, and exercises accompany the grammatical explanation.

A usage section is included for grades 8, 9, and 10, and a review of punctuation for grade 11.

The unit for grade 12 includes instruction on writing forcefully as well as supplementary exercises on the topics learned in grades 8 to 12.

The grade levels are colour coded for accessibility and interest.

How to Use *Talking about Writing*

This text is intended to provide a **finite amount of essential information** for the designated grade. There is light at the end of the tunnel.

In contrast to the leisurely musing which characterizes the composing process, or the angular discussion which accompanies literary analysis, **the pace of a language class is rapid**. Two to five minutes is adequate for a short Practice Exercise. It is left brain activity. Students are learning how to **organize and sharpen** their written work. So the teacher is encouraged to push forward quickly - not a wasted minute. 'Down time' encourages boredom. Keep the class at a gallop.

Language study is fun. **Every exercise is a puzzle**. Encourage the students to play with the concepts. Be patient with 'wrong' answers. Support inquisitiveness. Allow for possibility. If students come away with some knowledge of the intricacies of the language, and some respect for the ways it may be shaped, then the class has achieved its objective.

Students may mark their own or others' work. The overhead projector may be used to demonstrate in sequence the various 'jobs' requested in the Practice Exercises; for example, underline, circle, and draw arrows. Each 'job' may be given one mark and then the Practice Exercise scaled down by division to a reasonable worth. Encourage neatness and the use of a ruler.

At the conclusion of each sentence structure, grammar, or punctuation topic, students are asked to memorize certain aspects and to write definitions in their notebooks. In this way they keep their own record of what they have practised and have study material for tests.

Table of Contents for Grades 8 to 12 Programme

The *Answer Key* to chapters one to fifteen of *Talking about Writing* is available
as a separate text.

Chapter Four

Grade 9

Lack of Parallel Structure

I. Pre-test on Parallel Structure
If any of the following sentences is incorrect, rewrite it appropriately.

1. I enjoy eating, playing snooker, and hikes.
2. My brother likes sleeping late, borrowing my shirts, and to give me a hard time.
3. He skips not only his own chores but also bothers me when I am trying to do mine.
4. One day I am going to win a million dollars, leave home, and then I will never be bothered by my brother again.
5. Is this a pipe-dream, a possibility, or am I just thinking negatively?
6. Swimming is better exercise than to jog.
7. British Columbia is famous for its mountains, its rivers, and you can also see extensive wildlife.
8. To unlock the old trunk was difficult but examining the contents was fun.
9. Janice does her craft with care, precisely and lovingly.
10. They pay neither rent nor help with the housework.

II. Definition of Parallel Structure
When a sentence contains two or more constructions that are equal in value or similar in function, they should be parallel, ie., **balanced in form**.

Problem 1:   • Our dog is large, curious, and has an even temper.

Format: • Our dog is
                    1) <u>large,</u>
                    2) <u>curious,</u>
           and 3) <u>has an even temper</u>.

The adjectives *large* and *curious* are not parallel to the third construction which contains the verb *has*.

Solution: • Our dog is
                    1) <u>large,</u>
                    2) <u>curious,</u>
           and 3) <u>even-tempered.</u>

In this case the adjective *even-tempered* is created to parallel the other two adjectives.

State a second solution. Which of the two solutions do you prefer? Why?

Problem 2:   • Our dog catches mice, barks dutifully at approaching strangers, and never refuses a romp.

Format: • Our dog
        1) <u>catches</u> mice,
        2) <u>barks</u> dutifully at approaching strangers,
  and 3) never <u>refuses</u> a romp.

In this case the verbs are parallel, but the first two constructions are positive in nature while the third is negative.

Solution: • Our dog
        1) <u>catches</u> mice,
        2) <u>barks</u> dutifully at approaching strangers,
  and 3) <u>jumps</u> at the chance to play.

In this case the third statement has been written positively to parallel the first two.

Give a second solution. State which you prefer and why.

Note that adjectives, adverbs and phrases, as in the examples above, do not damage the parallel structure **if** they are merely additional descriptive words.

III. Practice with Parallel Structure
Using the numbered format suggested in the previous examples, rewrite the following sentences. Underline the parts of speech that you have made parallel.

1. The cherries on the trees were red, juicy, and had fully ripened.
2. The robins discovered them and are flocking there for meals and snacks.
3. We decided we had better pick the fruit quickly, freeze it for winter, and not be robbed by the birds.
4. Joe chose the taller, sweet cherry tree, I selected the shorter, sour cherry tree, and the cats were keeping us company on the nearby fence.
5. They spent their time falling from the fence rails, chasing grasshoppers, and they sniffed at the cherries in pails on the ground.
6. The branches scraped against our arms, poked into our backs, and knock us on the head when we move.
7. Watching robins chattered with disapproval and worriedly as we despoiled their trees.
8. They felt like residents and they also prey on garden bugs.
9. We could not help laughing at how frustrated they felt, their antics and sauciness.
10. To climb a cherry tree, surround oneself with pungent fruit, and eating as one picks is fun.

In your notebook write a definition for parallel structure and give an example.

IV. Practice with Parallel Structure using Correlative Conjunctions
A. Definition of Correlative Conjunction

A **correlative conjunction** is a **pair of coordinate conjunctions**. (See Grade 8, pg. 6.) A correlative conjunction, therefore, also joins constructions of **equal value** in a sentence; such as, **single words**, **phrases**, and **sentences**.

The correlative conjunctions are *either - or*, *neither - nor*, *not only - but also*, and *both - and*.

Problem: • You will either clean up your room or you will be grounded.

Format: • You will
   either 1) <u>clean up</u> your room
   or   2) you <u>will be grounded</u>.

Note that Part 1) of the structure has no subject while Part 2) contains a subject, *you*.

Solution: • *Either*
   1) <u>you will clean up</u> your room
   • *or*   2) <u>you will be grounded</u>.

In this case Part 1) has been given the subject *you* to parallel the subject in Part 2).

Note that a method of attaining parallel structure while using correlative conjunctions is to move one word in the pair - the word *either*, for example - to different places within the sentence and to check the effect.

Moving the word *either* in this way also allows the elimination of words that have been repeated in **both** Part 1) and Part 2) and may not be essential to the writer's purpose.

Format a second solution to the problem sentence. State which solution you prefer and why.

Practice Exercise 1

Using the format given in the previous example, correct the lack of parallel structure in the following sentences. Underline the parallel constructions.

1. Ben is neither enamoured of vacuuming nor getting meals.
2. We not only lost our motor but also James forgot the tackle box.
3. Every day he both attends the matinee and the evening performance.
4. She will either have to sew her dress today or she will have to wear her old one.
5. We can neither find my sister nor the keys to the car.
6. Sara is not only responsible for the lighting but also for the programme.
7. Each day he both sorts the letters and the parcels.
8. The buck will either run from the other male or they will fight for dominance.
9. I can neither eat chocolate nor nuts.
10. The children are not only creative but also they are cooperative.

In your notebook write a definition of correlative conjunction and give examples.

Memorize the four correlative conjunctions.

V. Post-test on Parallel Structure

Rewrite the following sentences so as to achieve parallel structure.
Use the format suggested.

1. They proceeded to take a bus to their hotel rather than driving.
2. His references will vouch that he is at ease with the public, can operate a till, and his attendance record is also excellent.
3. Immigrants are consumers of goods and services as well as they create work.
4. Her attendance and always being punctual have impressed her employer.
5. He started getting interested in the things she liked; such as, French, learning to meditate, and she played tennis as well.
6. The nurse was cheerful, helpful, and a friend to all.
7. The dog was either not mine or he had lost his sense of smell.
8. The train was never on time, always untidy, and noisy.
9. The beach is empty of people, littered with paper bags and bottles, and has an oily slick.
10. She is both attending the dinner and the dance.

In general, parallel structure eliminates unnecessary words and focusses the sentence.

Chapter Five

Grade 9

Misplaced Modifier

1. Pre-test on Misplaced Modifier
Rewrite any of the following sentences which may be incorrect.

1. The team nearly ate all of the cake; only one small piece remained.
2. I had almost driven to the mall when the car engine began to rattle.
3. He only wants his fair share.
4. The flowers brightened the room in a red vase.
5. We saw a man building a house with one leg.
6. A pearl was found by my sister in an oyster shell.
7. This lucky person has won a year's supply of peanut butter in jeans.
8. The house sits on a large lawn with a new coat of paint.
9. Humming-birds should not be fed after July in this part of the world.
10. Her friend sent her a necklace for Christmas in a velvet box.

II. Definition of Misplaced Modifier
A **misplaced modifier** is a **single word** or **phrase** which is incorrectly positioned in the sentence and therefore appears to modify (describe) the wrong word.

A. Single words which may be incorrectly positioned include *only*, *nearly*, and *almost*.

Example 1:   • Of all the seafoods he only eats shrimp.

In this sentence the adverb *only* modifies the verb *eats*.
In reality the person may do other things in his life besides eat. He does not only eat.
Therefore, the word *only* is more appropriate as an adjective modifying the noun *shrimp*.

Correction: • Of all the seafoods he eats **only** **shrimp**.

B. Adjective and adverb phrases may also appear to modify the wrong word.

Example 2:   • He ran to the station in green pyjamas.

The phrase *in green pyjamas* is positioned beside the noun *station* and therefore appears to describe it.
The sentence is more appropriately written so as to have the phrase *in green pyjamas* modify the pronoun *he*.

Correction: • *In green pyjamas* he ran to the station.

III. Grammatical Explanation of Single Word Modifiers: Adjectives

A. Definition of Adjective
An **adjective** is a word used to modify (describe) a *noun* or *pronoun*.
An adjective answers the question *which?*

Example: • bear;   *a big, brown* bear

• *which* bear?   *a big, brown* bear!

B. Other forms in which adjectives may appear include the following:

• *one* bear;   *that* bear;   *my* bear;   *the* bear;   *Canadian* bear

• *a* bear, *big* and *brown,* roared.

C. The verb *to be* (*is, are, was, were, shall be, will be, has been, had been, have been,* etc.,) is followed by an adjective, a noun or a pronoun.

• the bear *is* big.   (adjective)

D. The *sense* verbs (*look, taste, sound, smell, feel)* are also followed by an adjective, a noun or a pronoun.

• the bear *looks* big.   (adjective)

E. Other such **verbs of *being or condition*** that similarly are completed by an adjective, a noun or a pronoun include *seem, appear, grow, become, turn.*

• the bear *seems* tall.   (adjective)

Note that the question *which?* is also answered by adjectives following the verb *to be,* the *sense* verbs, and verbs of *being* or *condition.*

In French these same verbs, sixteen in all, are conjugated with the verb *etre (to be)* instead of with the verb *avoir (to have).*

Practice Exercise 1

In the following sentences underline each adjective and draw an arrow to the noun or pronoun it modifies. In each case state the question that is answered by the adjective.

• The white horse galloped along the busy highway.

which horse?   *which* highway?
the white horse   *the busy* highway

1. The quiet barn smells of sweet, dry hay.
2. The square hay bales, solid and heavy, climb toward the rough rafters.
3. Occasional spaces between the bales create small hideaways.
4. Barn cats pop out unexpectedly to waylay passing feet.
5. A long rope tied to a sturdy beam gives a dizzy ride.
6. The air is golden with dancing dust.
7. Above the hay-strewn floor other beams are narrow footpaths beneath a sloping roof.
8. From this height the coloured world unravels to wide horizons.
9. The earth-bound climber becomes a fearless eagle.
10. The hay barn is an enchanted place.

Practice Exercise 2

Write 5 sentences using adjectives to describe such nouns as the following and draw an arrow to the word each adjective modifies:

lake	lunch	my room	sunset	main street
hockey	snow	movie	dreams	playground

In your notebook write a definition for adjective and state the question it answers. Give examples.

Memorize the definition for adjective.

IV. Grammatical Explanation of Single Word Modifiers: Adverbs

A. Definition of Adverb

An **adverb** is a word used to modify (describe) a *verb*, an *adjective*, or *another adverb*.
An adverb answers the question *how? when? where? why?* or *to what degree?*

Examples:

| come *later* | walk *home* | *very* hot | *too* quickly |
| v   adv | v   adv | adv adj | adv adv |

| come *when?* | walk *where?* | *how* hot? | *how* quickly? |
| | | | *to what degree?* |

B. Other forms which adverbs may take include the following:

- most words ending in *ly* are adverbs.
- the words *not* and *never* are adverbs.
- the words *yes, no, indeed, perhaps, therefore, consequently,*
  and *however* are adverbs.

Practice Exercise 1

In the following sentences underline each adverb, draw an arrow to the verb, the adjective, or the adverb it modifies, and state the question which the adverb answers.

- <u>Soon</u> the sailor hurried <u>hastily</u> <u>back</u> to his comfortable ship.

| hurried *when?* | hurried *how?* | hurried *where?* |
| hurried *soon* | hurried *hastily* | hurried *back* |

1. I walk outside early in the morning.
2. The horses trot briskly to the fence and whinny inquiringly at me.
3. They watch me closely as I carefully carry breakfast to the kittens in the barn.
4. They attempt to show clearly that they are exceedingly hungry.
5. As they dance skittishly, they snort loudly and toss their heads high in the air.
6. I am not very interested, however.
7. Their paddock is now heavily matted with plants that are completely edible.
8. Their coats shine brightly.
9. Their eyes sparkle winsomely.
10. As I enter the stable door, they toss their heads disgustedly and gallop far away.

Practice Exercise 2

Form adverbs from each of the following adjectives and use 5 of these adverbs in sentences.

true	real	sincere	fine	able
single	final	neat	large	busy

Practice Exercise 3

If possible, make an adjective and an adverb from each of the following nouns.

Noun	Adjective	Adverb
storm		
length		
brashness		
time		
finale		
perfection		
love		
fortune		
consequence		
interest		

C. Punctuation for Adverbs used as Parenthetical Expressions

A **parenthetical expression** is a word or phrase inserted as extra information and indicated by commas or brackets.   Examples are such words as *therefore* and *however.*

Therefore, consequently, and *however* are **adverbs**.

They are placed in a sentence in order to create a logical argument.
They are separated by commas from the rest of the sentence in order to show that they represent a parenthetical expression.

• Non-smoking flights, *therefore*, became the norm.
           s   v

• The smoking public, *consequently*, had to adjust their habits.
           s   v

• No reduction in ticket sales, *however*, was recorded.
    s   v   v

However, when these words are used to introduce a second sentence which is closely related to the preceding sentence, then *a semicolon and a comma* must be used *in order to avoid a run-on sentence.*

- Bus lines also introduced non-smoking runs; *therefore,* non-smoking passengers

  s   v   s

  travelled in comfort.

  v

- The public were encouraged to request further non-smoking areas;

  s   v   v

  consequently, public offices accommodated this trend.

  s   v

- Smoking is generally acknowledged to be detrimental to health;

  s   v   v

  however, groups of people continue to smoke.

  s   v

Practice Exercise 4

Using commas and semicolons, punctuate the following sentences.

1. The plants in the window are beginning to droop consequently they require water.
2. Following the fire however the house was not rebuilt.
3. The computer program at first seemed promising however a more advanced version soon appeared.
4. Near the top of the hill therefore a satellite dish was erected.
5. I am finished therefore I am leaving.
6. The younger siblings consequently were imaginative.
7. Place the muffins in the oven however avoid jarring the pan or they may fall.
8. The trees therefore spread their branches widely.
9. The bird-feeder had been in service for a week however no birds had visited it.
10. Therefore the cat lost interest in the site.

In your notebook write a definition for adverb and state the questions which it answers. Give examples.

Memorize the definition for adverb.

V. Grammatical Explanation of Prepositional Phrase Modifiers

A. Definition of Prepositional Phrase
A **prepositional phrase** is a group of words beginning with a preposition.
A preposition is a *location* word; such as, *in, to, into, at, of, from, beyond, over, under, inside, outside, through, above, below, against.*

A prepositional phrase usually follows the **pattern**

or
- *preposition, adjective, noun*
- *preposition, pronoun*

B. A typical prepositional phrase, therefore, would occur as follows:

- He went *into the store.*

C. Any number of adjectives may occur and *not* disrupt the pattern:

- He went *into the large, airy, department store.*

D. English language removes the *the, a,* or *an* before the pronoun:

- He tripped *over me.*

E. Occasionally idiomatic expressions call for *preposition, noun* (no adjective). An idiomatic expression is a particular usage which everyone accepts over time.

- She arrived *on time.*

- He left *by car.*

Practice Exercise 1
In the following sentences circle the prepositions and underline the prepositional phrases.

• The water washed (over) the sidewalk and (into) the yard.

1. The boy in the brown suit leaped over the fence.
2. The group will meet outside the building on the corner of Main Street and First Avenue.
3. I meet my dad for lunch on Fridays.
4. To my surprise a bird in a tuxedo landed on the lawn.
5. With a yell the cub master awakened his troop from sleep.
6. The doll in the tutu has been listed for sale.
7. Gleefully she dashed into the house.
8. The horse rolled exuberantly among the wild poppies.
9. Through the long night the father sat by the sick child's bed.
10. The snow fell softly upon the dark branches.

In your notebook write a definition for preposition and give examples.
Memorize the definition for preposition.

VI. Types of Prepositional Phrase
Prepositional phrases may be subdivided into two types:
adjective phrase and **adverb phrase**.

A. An **adjective phrase** does the same work as an adjective.
It modifies a noun or pronoun and answers the question *which?*

• The girl *in the brown dress* is my sister.

Which girl? The girl *in the brown dress*

Therefore, *in the brown dress* is an adjective phrase and modifies the noun *girl.*

B. An **adverb phrase** does the same work as an adverb.
It modifies a verb, an adjective, or another adverb and answers the question *how, when, where, why,* or *to what degree?*

• He jumped *over the snake.*

He jumped *where?*
He jumped *over the snake.*

Therefore, *over the snake* is an adverb phrase and modifies the verb *jumped.*

44

Note that sometimes a phrase *appears* to be answering the question *where?* and modifying the verb when it more appropriately is answering the question *which?* and modifying the noun.

Example 1:

or

Example 2:

- The old house across the street burned down.

- The old house burned down across the street.

which old house?
the old house *across the street*

If one tries to make the phrase *across the street* answer the question *where?*, as it appears at first glance to do, then one creates the impression that the house may burn down *across the street* today and at another location tomorrow.

Therefore, Example 2 may be accused of containing a misplaced modifier.

It is wise, therefore, to be aware of prepositional phrases in a sentence so as to make sensible decisions about their location.

Practice Exercise 2

In the following sentences circle the prepositions and underline the prepositional phrases. State the question each phrase answers, identify the type of prepositional phrase, and draw an arrow to the word which the phrase modifies.

- The garden (at) the back (of) the house lay (in) shadow.
        adj   adj   adv

which garden?   *which* back?   lay *where?*
at the back   *of the house*   *in shadow*

1. The car in the alley was decorated with streamers.
2. The baseball team from town boarded the bus in the early morning.
3. The packages on the counter were wrapped in twine and labelled with felt pen.
4. The trip was advertised in the newspaper and on radio.
5. He tackled the project with enthusiasm and completed it on time.
6. The swimmer in Lane 6 was gasping for breath.
7. Place the food on the tray and cover it with a clean cloth.
8. With a smile the student stepped to the podium.
9. The jeans on the rack were discounted by fifty per cent.
10. By daybreak the wind had risen to one hundred kilometres an hour.

In your notebook write definitions for adjective phrase and adverb phrase and give examples. **Memorize** these definitions.

C. Punctuation Rule for Long Introductory Prepositional Phrases

A **long** introductory prepositional phrase must be separated from the rest of the sentence by a comma.

> • *At* the head *of* a long row *of* stationary vehicles, a white Porsche had rear-ended a Chevrolet van.

Note that *two or three* prepositional phrases constitute a "long" introduction.

A *short* introductory prepositional phrase, however, is **not** separated from the rest of the sentence by a comma.

> • *Inside* their motionless vehicles the drivers fumed.

Practice Exercise 3

Punctuate appropriately the following sentences. Give your reasons.

1. Above the long lines of moving vehicles a traffic helicopter circled.
2. The voice of the traffic reporter could be heard on the car radios.
3. Beside the roads police cars surveyed the morning rush into the city.
4. At the south end of the Port Mann bridge a three-car collision added to the frustration.
5. On the outgoing lanes traffic proceeded quickly.
6. At a distance the city appeared peaceful.
7. Against a backdrop of blue sky the buildings were clearly visible.
8. Above them wheeled screeching sea-gulls.
9. Along the roofs and ledges pigeons paraded stiffly.
10. Into the welcoming throng of people and birds the traffic advanced.

VII. Post-test on Misplaced Modifier

Rewrite the following sentences to avoid misplaced modifiers.

1. The man is eating pie with a pipe.
2. The hotel was full of my friends, cheaply built, highly combustible, and inadequately staffed.
3. A grey rabbit was found in our lane which had special markings on it.
4. My family has received a basket of fruit from our new neighbours, some of which are the juiciest I have ever seen.
5. We are nearly fond of all large dogs.
6. This lane leads to my friend's house that is now in Alberta.
7. She had almost eaten the entire salad when she noticed the pencilled note: *For the Party.*
8. Stella only had the right response.
9. Wanted: a boy to mow lawns under sixteen years of age.
10. Mom wants the person's name that left the mess in the bathroom.

VIII. Sentence Combining: Practice with Modifiers called *Words in Apposition*

A. Definition of Words in Apposition, or Appositives
Apposition means *positioned side by side.*

Words in apposition, therefore, are words placed beside a noun or pronoun which give extra information about the noun or pronoun.

B. Words in apposition are *preceded and followed by a comma.*
These commas act like **little hooks**. In your imagination you may put your fingers through these commas and **hook** the extra information **out** of the sentence without damaging the completeness of the part that remains.

- The snow, soft and white, looked like talcum powder.

    soft and white

The snow looked like talcum powder.

Note that words in apposition may occur at the beginning or end of a sentence as well as in the middle.
- *Soft and white*, the snow looked like talcum powder.
- The snow looked like talcum powder, *soft and white*.
- The snow, *soft and white*, looked like talcum powder.

Note that in the first two examples a second comma is not possible either at the beginning of the sentence where the capital letter sits or at the end of the sentence where a period must be placed. In all three examples, however, the extra information is still hooked out.

Practice Exercise 1
In each of the following sentences, underline the words in apposition.
Draw an arrow from the words in apposition to the noun or pronoun about which they are giving extra information.

Remember that sometimes a participle acts as a noun or an adjective. See 5 and 6 below.

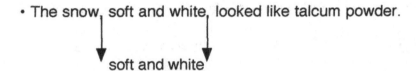
- A small puppy, the runt of the litter, tottered across the floor.

1. Sandy, my youngest sister, wants to do everything I do.
2. A little pest, she manages to discover any plans I have in mind.
3. She senses whenever I want to take a walk, my least significant outing.
4. She also knows instinctively when I have big plans, a cruise around town.
5. Whining and snivelling, she appears out of nowhere, four and a half feet of glue.

6. I try ignoring her, a useless exercise, or yelling at her, wasted effort.
7. Then mom appears, her champion.
8. She hands Sandy a list, a page of errands, "which you may as well do, since you're already going downtown."
9. Flabbergasted and disgusted, I stand disbelievingly, keys of my getaway car in my hand.
10. A prisoner of fate, I silently lead the way to the garage; my sister, the demon, trailing triumphantly at my heels.

C. Words in apposition are an excellent method of sentence combining because they combine short, choppy sentences and eliminate unnecessary subjects and verbs.

Example: • My sister is a lawyer. She works in Ottawa.

Solution: • My sister, **a lawyer,** works in Ottawa.

Note that combining the two sentences eliminates the verb *is* and the subject *she.*

D. Sentence Combining Method using Words in Apposition

Look in the sentences for the two things that are the same.
Put a comma at each end of the group of words that represents *extra* information and combine the two sentences into one.

Remember that *either* group of words may represent extra information. Therefore, there are always **two ways** of using words in apposition to combine sentences. One, however, may seem more sensible than the other.

Words in apposition *must* have two commas (or equivalent) or else the extra information remains *stuck* to the noun or pronoun.

Practice Exercise 2
Using words in apposition and appropriate punctuation, combine each of the following groups of short, choppy sentences into one smooth sentence.

1. Jane is my sister. She lives in Enderby.
2. Jones is our neighbour. He builds cedar canoes.
3. Arthur is a superb cook. He is catering our next 4-H banquet.
4. My sister plays goalie. She is the tall girl with red hair.
5. Penelope is the most daring equestrian. She is riding the Arabian.
6. My dad will show you the ropes. He is the boss on this ranch.

7. Thunder is a drum concert. The sound terrifies our dog.
8. The baby robin hops purposefully across the lawn after his mother. He is a fat and pampered youngster.
9. He opens his mouth wide. It is a red cave. The cave seems to extend right down to his tail.
10. His voice is a childish cheep. It echoes across the lawn.

E. Punctuation for Other Forms of Words in Apposition

1. Words in apposition introduced by *or* also require commas.

   - In Canada the buffalo, **or bison,** is largely extinct.

2. *Contrasting* expressions introduced by *not* require commas.

   - They were alarmed, ***not* by the isolation,** but by visitors.

   Note that the sentence that remains after the removal of a "contrasting expression" is not so clearly complete.

3. *Restrictive* words in apposition do not take commas because the information provided by them is essential to the sense of the sentence.

   - The skater Cranston represented Canada.

   (**Not**   The skater, Cranston, represented Canada.)

Practice Exercise 3
Punctuate appropriately the following forms of words in apposition.

1. The painting a water-colour of the Queen Charlotte Islands hung in the foyer of the bank.
2. The artist Jackson had been commissioned to do the work.
3. The picture was interesting not for the scene itself but for the quality of the light.
4. A rocky peninsula or strand jutted into a turbulent sea.
5. Above wheeled sea-gulls tireless and remote.
6. A woman a street person stood silently regarding the painting.
7. She was remarkable not for her beauty but for her presence.
8. She paid no attention to the crowd or melee which surged past her.
9. Bank Manager Martin watched her with interest.
10. He felt that she was experiencing his own reaction to the painting a sense of isolation.

In your notebook write a definition for words in apposition, or appositives, and give examples.

Memorize the definition for words in apposition, or appositives.

IX. Grade 9 Punctuation Summary

The following sentences assess punctuation learned in Grade 8 in connection with run-on sentences and sentence fragments as well as punctuation learned in connection with modifiers.

Punctuate appropriately. Be ready to give reasons for the punctuation you choose.

1. In the early hours of the morning the house is quiet.
2. Because no one is moving about the hum of the refrigerator seems loud.
3. Outside the dew is heavy on the grass and the feet of small animals leave trails in the wet.
4. Sunlight a gentle yellow warmth brightens the paint on buildings.
5. It slants across the street and colours deep shadows in the wake of obstacles.
6. It touches the faces of boxed red geraniums on window-sills and glints from tumbling green plants in rockeries.
7. An early riser comes into view clatters along the sidewalk and disappears around the next corner.
8. He is unusual not in appearance but in energy as the rest of the neighbourhood seems asleep.
9. Suddenly a street-sweeper or water truck rumbles heavily along the asphalt it sprays hot water while its brushes churn up the debris.
10. The driver enjoys the sensation he creates consequently he gears up and down with gusto.
11. The effect however is not conducive to slumber.
12. The community Westvale grudgingly awakes.

X. Syntax for Grade 9

Knowing the functions of nouns, verbs, adjectives and adverbs in a sentence enables one to use new words correctly.

Fill in the blanks below to create a coherent paragraph.

> • The _____ works in this way: _____ the _____ to the _____, but do so _____ because the _____ wheel has to _____ toward the _____. If the _____ is _____, then _____ the outside of the _____ as close to the _____ panel as possible. Turn the washer in a _____ direction and _____ for the best.

Practice Exercise 4

Write a paragraph and leave blanks for nouns, verbs, adjectives and adverbs.
Exchange with a partner and fill in the blanks.
Discuss.

Chapter Six

Grade 9

Usage

I. Pre-test One on Correct Use of Pronouns
Choose the correct form of the pronoun.

1. They are faster than (I, me).
2. Everybody was on time except (we, us).
3. It must have been (he, him).
4. When will you and (she, her) arrive?
5. I can do as well as (he, him).
6. Wait for Tom and (I, me).
7. They realized it was (she, her).
8. Hockey is a favourite sport with (we, us) Canadians.
9. For (who, whom) are you making that picture?
10. The children found (whoever, whomever) was hiding.
11. We know that fact as well as (they, them).
12. Who is it? It is (he, him).
13. Give an extra helping to David and (I, me).
14. Paul told (she, her) and (I, me) to give a hand.
15. (Who, Whom) does she resemble?

II. General Information on Case of Pronouns
The *relation* of certain pronouns to other words in the sentence determines the *form* in which the pronouns are written.

• *I* or *me*	• *she* or *her*	• *he* or *him*
• *we* or *us*	• *they* or *them*	• *who* or *whom*

The forms which must be learned for correct usage are the pronouns in the nominative case and the pronouns in the objective case.

The **nominative case** applies to times that a pronoun acts as a *subject* or a *subjective completion*.

The **objective case** applies to times that a pronoun acts as an *object of a verb* or an *object of a preposition*.

Therefore, the first goal is to recognize a subject, an object, and a subjective completion.

III. Subject of a Verb
A. Definition
The subject is the *doer* of the action; the verb is the *action*.

• She reached the summit of the hill.
    s   v

Practice Exercise 1
In each sentence place *s* under the subject and *v* under the verb.

1. I found the hidden candy.
2. We slid the game under the sofa.
3. You attached the rope to the wrong branch.
4. They appeared out of nowhere.
5. She could not see the point of the conversation.

IV. Direct Object of a Verb
A. Definition

The direct object of a verb *receives directly the action from the verb.*

> • Sam hit [the ball.]
>   s   v   object

1. Note that nothing intruded between the verb *hit* and the ball.
The ball **felt** that hit.

2. Slam your hand against the desktop.

> • My hand hit [the desktop.]
>   s   v   object

Note that nothing intruded between the verb *hit* and the desktop.
Your hand **felt** the desktop; probably the desktop felt your hand!

3. This point may be illustrated by the diagram below:

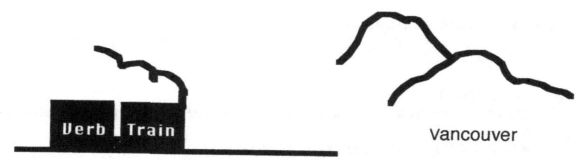

Vancouver

The verb train is chugging down the track to its object, Vancouver.
Nothing intrudes between the verb train and its object, Vancouver.
The verb train will chug straight to Vancouver because nothing is on the track.

Practice Exercise 2
Following the pattern given above, find the subject and the verb and box the direct object.
Note that *all* adjectives associated with the object are included in the box.

1. The ball smashed the laboratory window.
2. Scalpers sold football tickets.
3. The fog enveloped the town.
4. They did not reveal the secret.
5. He sewed the torn pocket.

Note that the subject and the object are **two completely different things**.

In your notebook write a definition for subject of verb and object of verb. Draw the verb train to illustrate your definitions.

V. Subjective Completion of a Verb
A. Definition

A subjective completion completes the information about the subject.
It is *the same as* or *describes* the subject.

Example 1:   • My sister is $\boxed{\text{a nurse.}}$
                     s   v   subjective completion

Note that *my sister* and *a nurse* are **the same thing**.

Example 2:   • This cake tastes $\boxed{\text{good.}}$
                     s   v   subjective completion

Note that the the word *good* **describes** *cake.*

Practice Exercise 3
Following the pattern given above, find the subject and the verb and box the subjective completion.
Remember to include all descriptive words associated with the completion.

1. Pearl is a good high jumper.
2. Trudy seems happy.
3. Today Thomasina became a pilot.
4. Those pies smell delicious.
5. The boys are buddies.

VI. General Notes on Object and Completion

A. The pattern of sentences containing an object and a completion *appears* the same.

However, when you look to see if the subject and the object are *different* or *related*, then you can distinguish the object from the completion.

B. Verbs which take a *subjective completion* include the following:

- the verb **to be** in all its forms: *is, are, was, were, has been, had been, will be;*

- the **"sense" verbs**: *to look, to feel, to smell, to taste, to sound;* and

- **verbs of condition**; such as, *to appear, to become, to seem, to turn.*

Memorize these verbs.

Practice Exercise 4

Using the pattern developed in the previous exercises, label the subject *s* and the verb *v*, and box and label the object or completion.

1. The cow kicked the coyote.
2. My brother was ecstatic.
3. Mom lets us.
4. The prisoner gained his freedom.
5. That child is a nuisance.
6. Soon he will be a graduate.
7. Today Harvey sounds appreciative.
8. She found the answer.
9. The elephant crushed the ant.
10. The apples turned redder.
11. The car struck the signpost.
12. She became quite defensive.
13. The laundry smelled sour.
14. The woman selected the cheese.
15. They have been asleep.

In your notebook write a definition for subjective completion.
Show how object of a verb is different from subjective completion of a verb.

VII. Object of a Preposition

Look at the verb train in the diagram below:

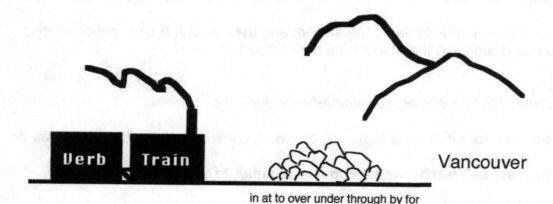

in at to over under through by for
of from into beyond with

Note the pile of rocks on the track.

Each of those rocks is a **preposition** preventing the train from getting through to its destination, Vancouver.

Therefore, from the verb train's point of view, Vancouver has become an **indirect object** because the verb train cannot get past the rocks.

From Vancouver's point of view, it is now **looking at rocks** instead of at the verb train. Therefore, Vancouver has become **the object of the preposition**.

• I went (to) [the store.]
  s   v   object of the preposition

Practice Exercise 5

Following the pattern given above, label the subject *s* and the verb *v*, circle the preposition (the rock), and box and label the object of the preposition.

1. He tripped over the electrical cord.
2. A glorious rainbow arched above the town.
3. They worked past midnight.
4. The puck slid into the net.
5. They asked for a refund.
6. He went to bed.
7. The answer is located in the back.
8. The animals ran behind the barn.
9. The fog stretched beyond the city.
10. The children ran around the playground.

Memorize these prepositions.

VIII. Case of Pronouns

A. Since a pronoun takes the place of a noun, a pronoun can do whatever a noun can.

1. Therefore, both a noun and a pronoun may be **subject of a verb**

   • *Sam* hit the ball.   • *He* hit the ball.

2. Both a noun and a pronoun may be **subjective completion of a verb**

   • Sam is a *fire ball*.   • A fire ball is *he*.

3. Both a noun and a pronoun may be **object of a verb**

   • The ball hit *Sam*.   • The ball hit *him*.

4. Both a noun and a pronoun may be **object of a preposition**

   • The grass is under *Sam*.   • The grass is under *him*.

B. A pronoun *differs* from a noun in that some pronouns change their *form* according to their *function* in the sentence as subject, object, or completion.

This change is called the **case** of the pronoun.

C.   **When Function of Pronoun is**   **then Case of Pronoun is**
         Subject of a verb   Nominative Case
         Subjective Completion of a verb   Nominative Case
         Object of a verb   Objective Case
         Object of a preposition   Objective Case

In your notebook write the four functions which a (noun or) pronoun may have in a sentence.

List the case of the (noun or) pronoun during each of these functions.

D. The *two types of pronoun* which change their form according to their function in the sentence are **personal** pronouns and some **relative** pronouns.

Personal pronouns stand for the names of persons, places, or things.

> • *She* (Mary) is a friend.   *(She stands for the name Mary.)*

Relative pronouns relate (refer) to nouns that have already been mentioned in a sentence.

> • We saw several people *whom* we knew.   *(Whom refers to people.)*

Personal Pronouns

Nominative Case	Objective Case
I	me
you (singular)	you (singular)
he, she	him, her
we	us
you (plural)	you (plural)
they	them

Relative Pronouns

Nominative Case	Objective Case
who	whom
whoever	whomever

In your notebook copy this chart showing the nominative case and the objective case of the personal pronouns and the relative pronouns.

Memorize this chart.

Practice Exercise 6
Choose from each bracket the correct form of the pronoun.
State the reason for your choice in terms of its function in the sentence and its case.

Example:	• He is taller than (I, me).
Solution:	• He is taller than **I** (am).

Subject of the implied verb *am*, nominative case.

Remember that a question must be turned into a statement for purposes of analysis:

• *Did you see that car?* becomes **You did see that car.**

1. Wait for Joe and (I, me).
2. You and (she, her) will clean up your rooms.
3. He knew it was (we, us).
4. What were you and (he, him) talking about?
5. She invited (he, him) and (I, me) to go driving.
6. It must have been (they, them).
7. I guessed the tall woman to be (she, her).
8. For (who, whom) is this parcel?
9. (Whoever, whomever) wishes may come.
10. Give the last piece to (whoever, whomever) you choose.
11. They are slower than (we, us).
12. They saw it was (he, him).
13. The kite was made by Sandra and (I, me).
14. Everyone is going except you and (she, her).
15. You golf as well as (he, him).

IX. Post-test One on Usage: Case in Pronouns
Choose the correct form of the pronoun.

1. (He, Him) exhibited his art.
2. The culprits were (she, her) and (I, me).
3. Mother gave (he, him) and (she, her) some supper.
4. The winners are (we, us) or (they, them).
5. (Who, Whom) are you taking with you?
6. (We, us) girls are going skating.
7. This dress suits her better than (I, me).
8. Give one to (whoever, whomever) you see.
9. Who was it? It was (she, her).
10. She is older than (he, him).

I. Pre-test Two on Transitive and Intransitive Verb
Choose the correct form of the verb.

1. Let her (lie, lay) quietly.
2. That seam has never (lain, laid) flat.
3. The man (lay, laid) down gratefully.
4. The instructions said to (lie, lay) it down, and I (lay, laid) it down.
5. The dog (lay, laid) in the same spot for several minutes.
6. Suddenly he remembered seeing the money (lying, laying) on the shelf.
7. (Sit, Set) here and chat.
8. Last night we (sat, set) around and played cards.
9. She (sat, set) the eggs in a separate bag.
10. (Sit, Set) a good example for your brother.
11. When do you want to (rise, raise)?
12. The price of meat has (raised, risen) recently.
13. She (rose, raised) herself on her elbow.
14. They (rose, raised) before dawn.
15. Insurgents may (rise, raise) in numbers.

II. Definition of Transitive and Intransitive Verb
Look again at the diagram of the verb train:

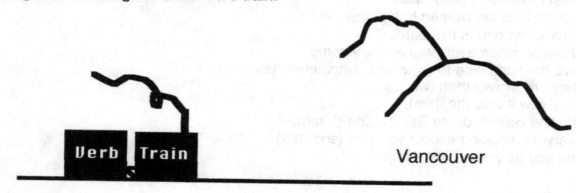

The prefix *trans* means *across*.

A verb in which action goes straight *across* to an object is called a *transitive verb*.

· Sam hit the ball.
 S   V

hit is a transitive verb because its action goes *across* to its direct object *the ball*.

Now look at the second diagram:

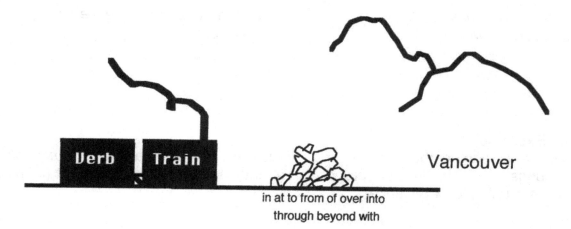

in at to from of over into
through beyond with

The prefix *intrans* means *not across.*

1. A verb in which action *cannot go* across to its object is called an *intransitive verb.*

• I went (to) the store.
  s   v

went is an intransitive verb because the preposition *to* sits between it and the object *store*.

2. An intransitive verb is also created by its having *no destination at all.*

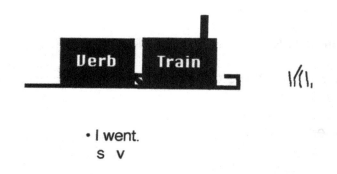

• I went.
  s   v

Adding descriptive words to the verb does not alter the intransitive verb.

• I went slowly.
  s   v   adv

III. Application

Transitive Verbs *(have an object)*
  lay (something down)
  set
  raise

Intransitive Verbs *(have no object)*
  lie (down)
  sit
  rise

Practice Exercise 1
Use in a sentence each of the transitive and intransitive verbs listed above. Put *s* under the subject, *v* under the verb, circle the preposition (if any), and box the direct object (if any). Check the verb trains for assistance.

Practice Exercise 2
Fill in the chart below. If you wish, use the pronoun *I*.

Infinitive	Simple Present	Simple Past	Present Participle	Past Participle
to lie (down)				
to lay (place)				
to sit				
to set				
to rise				
to raise				

Note that there is no such word as "lieing."

Practice Exercise 3
Choose the correct form of verbs *to lie* and *to lay*.

1. Even though it was raining, the boy ___ on the ground.
2. Every Saturday I ___ in bed until ten o'clock.
3. The treasure has ___ in the ground for centuries.
4. My grandfather was ___ down when we called.
5. The contractor has ___ the foundation for our house.
6. The store is ___ the groundwork for a sales promotion.
7. Yesterday we ___ around late.
8. Let it ___ there unseen.
9. Where did you ___ your dirty laundry?
10. The artist has ___ another colour on his palette.

Practice Exercise 4
Choose the correct form of each verb.

1. (Sit, set) the groceries on the counter.
2. (Sit, set) the timer for me.
3. I have been (sitting, setting) here alone.
4. The dog (sits, sets) in the road.
5. (Sit, Set) down.
6. Did you (rise, raise) the issue?
7. The moon has (rose, risen) above the trees.
8. They (rose, raised) early and ate.
9. The wind (rose, raised) the tarpaulin.
10. Each morning we (rose, raised) at seven.

IV. Post-test Two on Transitive and Intransitive Verb
Choose the correct form of the verb.

1. Wearily he (lay, laid) down on the bunk.
2. Having (laid, lain) down, the child refused to get up.
3. The dog (lay, laid) itself down close to the boy.
4. If you let garbage (lie, lay) for a while, it compacts.
5. The cap (lay, laid) yesterday in the same spot as it (lies, lays) today.
6. The prairies (lie, lay) to the east of British Columbia.
7. The choice (lies, lays) with you.
8. When school ended, I (lay, laid) my binders away.
9. The map had (laid, lain) unseen for years.
10. He (lies, lays) down at every opportunity.

V. Application to Dictionary Use

When a dictionary gives the meaning of a word, it indicates whether the verb is transitive or intransitive; *v.t.* or *v.i.*
This information tells the reader whether or not a preposition is needed to follow the verb.
This knowledge is essential to the correct use of an unfamiliar verb in a sentence.

> • He found the key. *(v.t.)*
> • He sat on it. *(v.i.)*

Practice Exercise 5
In the dictionary look up the meaning of the following verbs.
Note whether they are transitive or intransitive.
Use the verbs correctly in sentences.

> • fraternize • embroil • commandeer • stridulate • mirror

I. Pre-test Three on the Use of *Like* and *As*
Rewrite any of the following sentences which may be incorrect.

1. He ran like a rabbit.
2. The driver seemed like he knew where he was going.
3. Tell it like it is.
4. Buy one like mine.
5. This tastes good like a hamburger should.
6. She looked like she had seen a ghost.
7. Pitch it like you can!
8. They were acting like there was no tomorrow!
9. The daughter looks like her mother.
10. He speaks French like a native son.

II. The Difference between *Like* and *As*

A. *Like* is a *preposition*.
It introduces a prepositional phrase.

> • I dress *like* my friend.

> • My sister does not look *like* me.

Notice the *pattern* of a prepositional phrase:

> preposition, adjective, noun   *or*   preposition, pronoun

Practice Exercise 1
In each sentence circle the preposition and underline the prepositional phrase which the preposition introduces.

> • She sings (like) a bird.

1. These bills look like counterfeit money.
2. The band sounds like a professional group.
3. They appeared like magic.
4. The cake tastes like poppy seed torte.
5. He argues just like her.

B. As is a *conjunction.*
It introduces a subordinate clause.
A clause contains a subject and a verb.

• He sputtered (as) he spoke.
   s   v   s   v

• They reasoned in the same way (as) he (did).   (implied verb)
   s   v   s   v

Occasionally *as* will be part of a phrasal conjunction; such as, *as if, as though, as ___ as.*

Practice Exercise 2

In each sentence circle the conjunction and underline the subordinate clause.
Insert *s* and *v* under the subject and the verb.
If necessary, insert the implied verb, as in the above example.

1. My sister was as rough as her brother.
2. Play it as you can!
3. Our guest didn't stay up as late as we.
4. The hail enlarged as it fell.
5. The dishes looked as though they had not been washed.

Note that the use of the conjunction *as **if*** creates a *possibility*, not a fact. Therefore, the verb in the ensuing clause may take on the subjunctive mood. (See Grade 11, pages 125 to 127.)

Example: The girl felt **as if** she *were* dreaming.

III. Post-test Three on the Use of *Like* and *As*

Rewrite any of the following sentences which may be incorrect.

1. Do like he says, not like he does.
2. It looks like she is going to miss her ride.
3. If they work like beavers, they may finish on time.
4. The platform looked like it was going to break.
5. Daisies like miniature yellow suns line the road.
6. When the wind blows, the trees clap their leaves like hands.
7. She puts on her make-up thinly like me.
8. The kitten crouched like it was hunting.
9. The athlete limped like she was hurt.
10. Rose hips like red jelly beans on sticks shine from the hedge.

In your notebook write definitions to show the difference between *like* and *as* and give examples.

IV. Varying Sentence Structure: Further Application of Clauses
A. Definitions

1. A *clause* is a group of words containing a subject and a verb.

    • The osprey dived toward the water.
       s   v

    • When the osprey dived toward the water,
          s   v

2. A principal clause is a *complete idea*. It makes sense on its own.

    • The osprey dived toward the water.
       s   v

3. A subordinate clause is *not* a complete idea. It does not make sense on its own.

    • When the osprey dived toward the water,
          s   v

Note that a *subordinate conjunction* introduces a subordinate clause.
A subordinate conjunction turns a complete idea, or principal clause, into a subordinate clause.

    • *When* the osprey dived toward the water,

Examples of subordinate conjunctions include *as, when, while, if, because, since, although, which, that, who.*

Practice Exercise 3
Change each complete idea, or principal clause, into a subordinate clause by introducing it with a subordinate conjunction. Use as many different subordinate conjunctions as possible. Circle the subordinate conjunction and underline the subordinate clause twice.

1. The letter lay on the desk.
2. We need more peanut butter.
3. The score was tied.
4. The Cinderella fairy-tale is common to many races.
5. Dreams contain interesting symbolism.

Practice Exercise 4
Add a principal clause to each subordinate clause that you created in *Practice Exercise 3* in order to create a **complex sentence**.
Underline the principal clause once and the subordinate clause twice.

A *complex sentence* contains both a principal clause and a subordinate clause and is therefore more complex than a simple sentence, ie., a principal clause on its own.

• <u>As the letter lay on the desk</u>, <u>I was tempted to open it</u>.

Practice Exercise 5
Sometimes a subordinate clause "splits" a principal clause in two.

The subordinate conjunctions which introduce these subordinate clauses are the relative pronouns *which, that, who,* and *whom.*

These relative pronouns may act as the *subject* of the subordinate clause.

• <u>The apartment which was available was near a subway station</u>.
      s   s   v   v

Make each of the following subordinate clauses split a principal clause in two. Put **s** and **v** under the subject and verb in the principal clause, and **s** and **v** under the subject and verb in the subordinate clause. Circle the subordinate conjunction, and underline the subordinate clause twice.

1. that he noticed
2. which had a brown roof
3. whom she admired
4. that was required
5. who had suddenly arrived

Practice Exercise 6
Add a *coordinate conjunction* and a second principal clause to each principal clause below and thereby create a **compound sentence.**
Underline the principal clauses once and circle the coordinate conjunction.

Remember that the coordinate conjunctions are *and, but, or,* and *so.*   (See Grade 8, pg. 6.)

• The letter lay on the desk, (and) I was tempted to open it.
      S   V   S V V

1. My friend walked right past me.
2. The gravy became very thin.
3. Orange juice wakes me up quickly.
4. He was finally able to remember.
5. With a pop the light bulb burned out.

Practice Exercise 7
Change each of the following compound sentences into a complex sentence by subordinating one of the principal clauses.

1. The rain squall passed suddenly, and the sun came out strongly.
2. The girl looked at the hole in her stocking, and she grimaced.
3. Bartering is fairly common in some parts of the world, but it is less common in Canada.
4. The fish market is cheaper than retail outlets, so many people flock there to buy fresh fish.
5. The gift must be returned unused, or the store will not refund the money.

Practice Exercise 8
Change each of the following complex sentences into a compound sentence by removing the subordinate conjunction and inserting a coordinate conjunction.

1. When the band finally arrived, it was nearly eleven o'clock.
2. Because the topic was of interest, the hall was crowded.
3. Since the environment is the responsibility of everyone, many people are voicing their concern.
4. While the floor is wet, please use the back stairs.
5. If meat becomes too expensive, she may become a vegetarian.

Practice Exercise 9

Change each of the following compound or complex sentences into a simple sentence, ie., a principal clause.

• The wallpaper was blue.
      s   v

• The doors and windows were green.   (compound subject)
      s   s   v

• She took one look and left.   (compound predicate)
  s   v   v

1. As she listened to the story, she forgot her surroundings.
2. They cleaned the apartment, and they went out for a game of badminton.
3. After the team had been introduced to the school, they left for their first out-of-town game.
4. Either I take key-boarding this semester or I shall continue to hunt and peck.
5. The pudding tended to be damp in the middle, but nobody seemed to mind.

In your notebook write a definition for principal clause, subordinate clause, simple sentence, compound sentence, and complex sentence. Give an example of each.

I. Pre-test Four on General Usage

Rewrite any of the following sentences which may be incorrect.

1. The tenants sat between the ruins of their apartment block.
2. A certain amount of goals will get past even the most proficient goalie.
3. You have less mistakes on this assignment than on the last one.
4. Do good on this project and you won't have to write the final examination.
5. The team tries real hard but loses many games.
6. Allergies may effect one's choice of environment.
7. The last time we met was when you were twelve years old.
8. Fifteen dollars were all I could afford.
9. This meal is different than the one I had at the hotel.
10. If you except a favour from him, you will have to repay it.

II. Explanation

A. *Between* refers to the relationship of two objects.

> • The buyer cannot decide *between* these two brands.

Among refers to the relationship of more than two objects.

> • The cheerleaders sat *among* the spectators.

B. *Amount, Less* refer to a quantity that cannot be counted.

> • A small *amount* of grease was added to the pan.
> • *Less* opportunity for investment exists in these fields.

Number, Fewer refer to a quantity which can be counted.

> • A *number* of answers were incorrect.
> • *Fewer* birds migrate to the prairie sloughs.

C. *Good* is an adjective. The adverbial form is *well*.

> • He does *well* under stress.

To do good is an idiom which means *to be helpful to one's fellow beings.*

> • Many individuals have a reputation for *doing good.*

D. *Real* is an adjective.
The adverb is *really* and must be used to modify a verb, an adjective, or another adverb.

> • Mom was *really* surprised that the cookies disappeared so quickly.

E. In most circumstances *effect* is a noun and *affect* is a verb.

> • The *effect* of the drought will be felt for some time.
> • The torn tendon will *affect* his career in sports.

F. The verb *to be* is followed by a subjective completion, which may be a noun, a pronoun, or an adjective.
When, where, why are all subordinate conjunctions and therefore may **not** be used to complete the verb *to be.*

> • My worst experience was *the time* I wandered near a wasp nest.

G. A *collective noun* requires a singular verb when the objects named are considered as a unit.

> • Ten pounds *is* too small a crop.

H. The idiom **differ from** means *to be unlike.*

- Navel oranges taste *different from* tangerines.

I. Accept is a verb. **Except** is a preposition.

- Please *accept* my congratulations.
- *Except* for the skunk the animals are amiable.

III. Post-test Four on General Usage
Rewrite any of the following sentences which may be incorrect.

1. The bowl of popcorn sat among Derek and Craig.
2. The team gave up only a limited amount of goals.
3. Less broken eggs in wild bird nests are associated with lower levels of chemicals.
4. If my investments do good on the stock market, I shall consider philanthropy.
5. In low gear the motor turns over real slow.
6. Too much candy effects my complexion.
7. Basketball is when two teams try to put a ball in a hoop.
8. Five kilometres are the distance to the nearest town.
9. The wood in the desk is different than in the buffet.
10. Will the customer except a substitute article?

Works Consulted

For the material in this text I accessed three general sources: first, knowledge and skills which my elementary and secondary school teachers gave me when analysis of sentence structure and grammar were commonplace; second, early twentieth century texts on grammar and composition which I collected and enjoyed; and third, helpful books used during my teaching of secondary school English. The second and third sources I have listed below.

Buehler, Huber Gray, and Pelham Edgar. *A Modern English Grammar*. Toronto: Morang & Co. Limited, 1904.

Canadian Press Style Book. 1974.

Fowler, H.W. *A Dictionary of Modern English Usage*. London: Oxford University Press, 1949.

Irwin, H. W., and J.F. Every. *English Composition for High Schools*. Toronto: The Copp Clark Company, 1928.

Lang, S.E. *A Modern English Grammar*. Western Canada Series. Toronto: The Copp Clark Company, Limited, 1909.

Larock, Margaret H., Jacob C. Tressler, and Claude E. Lewis. *Mastering Effective English*. 4th ed. Toronto: Copp Clark Pitman, 1980.

Paton, J.M., and Allan D. Talbot. *The New Using Our Language*. Toronto: J.M. Dent & Sons, 1957.

Shaw, Harry. *Handbook of English*. 2nd Canadian ed. Toronto: McGraw-Hill Company of Canada Limited, 1970.

Stevenson, O.J. and H.W. Irwin. *High School English Composition*. Western Canada Series. Toronto: The Copp Clark Company, Limited, 1913.

Stevenson, O.J. and H.W. Kerfoot. *Ontario High School English Grammar*. Toronto: The Canada Publishing Company, Limited, 1929.

Strunk, William, Jr., and E.B. White. *The Elements of Style*. 3rd ed. New York: MacMillan Publishing Co. Inc., 1979.

Printed in the United States
by Baker & Taylor Publisher Services